The Bermuda Triangle

Jim Whiting

BERMUDA

ATLANTIC
OCEAN

Miami
FLORIDA

GULF OF
MEXICO

WITHDRAWN

Mitchell Lane
PUBLISHERS

P.O. Box 196
Hockessin, Delaware 19707
Visit us on the web: www.mitchelllane.com
Comments? email us:
mitchelllane@mitchelllane.com

San Juan
PUERTO RICO

Mitchell Lane PUBLISHERS

Printing   1   2   3   4   5   6   7   8   9

A Robbie Reader/Natural Disasters

The Ancient Mystery of Easter Island
The Bermuda Triangle
Bubonic Plague
Earthquake in Loma Prieta, California, 1989
The Fury of Hurricane Andrew, 1992
Hurricane Katrina, 2005
The Lost Continent of Atlantis
Mt. Vesuvius and the Destruction of Pompeii, A.D. 79
Mudslide in La Conchita, California, 2005
Tsunami Disaster in Indonesia, 2004
Where Did All the Dinosaurs Go?

Library of Congress Cataloging-in-Publication Data
Whiting, Jim, 1943–
　　The Bermuda Triangle / by Jim Whiting.
　　　　p. cm. — (A Robbie reader. Natural disasters)
　　Includes bibliographical references and index.
　　ISBN 1-58415-497-7 (library bound)
　　1. Bermuda Triangle—Juvenile literature. 2. Aircraft accidents—Bermuda Triangle—Juvenile literature. 3. Taylor, Charles, 1917–1945—Juvenile literature.
I. Title. II. Series.
　　G558.W55　2007
　　001.94—dc22
　　ISBN-10: 1-58415-497-7

2006006101
ISBN-13: 9781584154976

ABOUT THE AUTHOR: Jim Whiting has been a remarkably versatile and accomplished journalist, writer, editor, and photographer for more than 30 years. A voracious reader since early childhood, Mr. Whiting has written and edited about 200 nonfiction children's books. His subjects range from authors to zoologists and include contemporary pop icons and classical musicians, saints and scientists, emperors and explorers. Representative titles include *The Life and Times of Franz Liszt*, *The Life and Times of Julius Caesar*, *Charles Schulz*, *Charles Darwin and the Origin of the Species*, *Juan Ponce de Leon*, *Annie Oakley*, *Bubonic Plague*, and *The Scopes Monkey Trial*. He lives in Washington State with his wife and two teenage sons.

PHOTO CREDITS: Cover, pp. 1, 12—Sharon Beck; pp. 14, 16—Naval Historical Center; p. 4 (bottom)—Acey Harper/Time Life Pictures/Getty Images; p. 8—Florida State Archives; p. 10—Barbara Marvis; p. 11—Captain Albert E. Theberge, NOAA Corps; p. 15—Rear Admiral Harley D. Nygren, NOAA Corps; pp. 18, 20—NOAA; p. 21—NASA.

PLB

TABLE OF CONTENTS

Chapter One
The Flight to Nowhere 5

Chapter Two
Mystery and Legend 9

Chapter Three
Vanished—Into Thin Air? 13

Chapter Four
Some Explanations 19

Chapter Five
Is the Bermuda Triangle Real? 25

Chronology 28
Find Out More 30
    Books 30
    Works Consulted 30
    On the Internet 30
Glossary 31
Index 32

Words in **bold** type can be found in the glossary.

U.S. Navy torpedo bombers similar to the five ill-fated aircraft of Flight 19. The disappearance of Flight 19 is one of the most famous mysteries connected with the Bermuda Triangle.

The Fort Lauderdale airport, the place where Flight 19 took off. The planes never returned.

The Flight to Nowhere

On a bright sunny day, five U.S. Navy torpedo bombers roared down the runway in Fort Lauderdale, Florida. It was about 2:00 P.M. on December 5, 1945.

The group was known as Flight 19. The leader, Lieutenant Charles Taylor, was a very experienced pilot. The other four pilots didn't have as much experience. The flight was part of their advanced training. Four planes carried two crewmen besides the pilot. The fifth had one. The planes would fly a **triangular** course, most of it over water. The exercise was scheduled to last about two hours. The fourteen men expected to be back in plenty of time for dinner. They would never eat dinner again.

The first hint of trouble came about an hour and a half after takeoff. Lieutenant Taylor radioed, saying, "I don't know where we are. We must have got lost after that last turn." He said his compasses weren't working. He also thought he was flying over the Florida Keys, a series of small islands that extend west from the tip of Florida. Yet the planes had flown east, not west.

Soon Taylor said he had just passed a small island. There was no other land in sight. He was becoming more and more confused. He thought he was in the Gulf of Mexico, which is west of Florida. He turned east to reach the base.

He was wrong—the base was the other way. Time was running out. The planes were low on gas. The weather had changed, and the pilots could not see very far ahead of them. The wind was stronger, and the ocean was very rough.

Taylor's last message came in just after six o'clock. He said that the planes would have to ditch, or land in the open sea. No one ever heard from Taylor or the other pilots again.

Two big patrol planes roared into the air to look for the missing planes. Only one came back. The other one vanished. It carried 13 men.

Airplanes that vanish are big news for a while. Then people forget about them.

That didn't happen with Flight 19. It became famous. It is a central part of one of the world's best-known mysteries: the mystery of the Bermuda Triangle.

Earlier versions of the aircraft in Flight 19 soar over Miami, Florida, in 1941.

The Miami skyline in 1946. The airplane in the foreground is equipped with both floats and wheels. It could land on water or land.

Mystery and Legend

The **legend** of the Bermuda Triangle began in September 1950. Newspaper reporter E.V.W. Jones wrote an article about the many ships and airplanes that had disappeared off the coast of Florida. Hundreds of people had been lost. He added something else: There was no explanation for these disappearances.

Two years later, George X. Sand wrote an article in *Fate* magazine called "Sea Mystery at Our Back Door." He also talked about mysterious disappearances. He said many ships had vanished inside a large triangle. Its three corners were Florida, Bermuda, and Puerto Rico.

A few of the smaller Bermuda Islands. At about 1,000 miles east of the United States, the Bermudas make up one corner of the Bermuda Triangle.

Other people began writing stories about this region. In 1962, author Dale Milton Titler called it the "deadly triangle."

In 1964, Vincent Gaddis wrote a magazine article called "The Deadly Bermuda Triangle." This was the first time that the phrase *Bermuda Triangle* appeared in print. Gaddis's story was so popular, he wrote a book about the Bermuda Triangle.

Puerto Rico is another of the three points that make up the Bermuda Triangle. Christopher Columbus discovered Puerto Rico in 1493 and claimed it for Spain. This view of Puerto Rico's San Juan Harbor was taken in 1975.

Many more people explored the mysteries. They expanded the "triangle" into a different, larger shape. The larger size included even more mysterious vanishings.

Charles Berlitz wrote a very popular book in 1974. Called *The Bermuda Triangle*, it sold more than 5 million copies.

His book really put the Bermuda Triangle "on the map." People all over the country began talking about it.

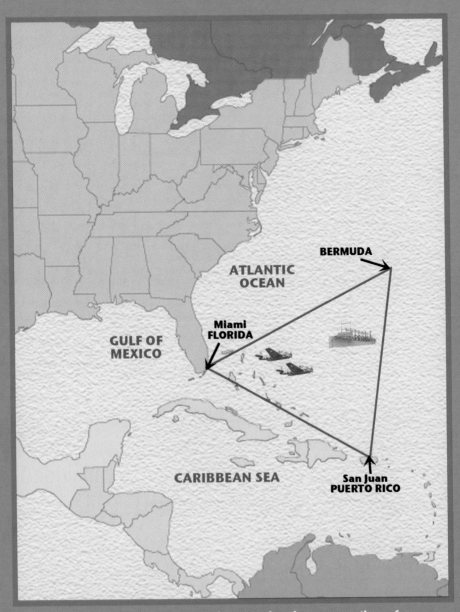

The Bermuda Triangle contains thousands of square miles of open ocean between Bermuda, San Juan, and Miami. Christopher Columbus noted mysterious occurrences here during his voyage to the New World in 1492. Since then, many other mysteries have been reported in the area.

Vanished—Into Thin Air?

Berlitz, like all the other writers, offered plenty of examples of disappearing ships and planes. Besides Flight 19, the most famous case concerns the USS *Cyclops*. It was a large U.S. Navy ship that carried coal. The ship sailed to Brazil early in 1918, then headed back toward the United States. It stopped briefly at Barbados (bar-BAY-duss), an island in the Caribbean Sea. No one ever saw the ship again. The U.S. Naval Historical Center says, "Her loss with all 306 crew and passengers, without a trace, is one of the sea's unsolved mysteries."

In 1948, an airliner called the *Star Tiger* was headed for Bermuda. Shortly before it was scheduled to land, the pilot sent a radio message. Then the plane disappeared.

The disappearance of the USS *Cyclops* is one of the most baffling mysteries connected with the Bermuda Triangle. The vessel was launched in 1910 and sank without a trace eight years later.

A committee of experts examined the disappearance. It concluded: "No more baffling problem has ever been presented."

Almost exactly a year later, an identical airplane called the *Star Ariel* left Bermuda and vanished without a trace. Three weeks before the loss of *Star Ariel,* a DC-3 airliner took off from Puerto Rico. Its destination was Miami.

A DC-3 airliner in 1949 like the one that disappeared on its way to Miami. The DC-3 is one of the most famous airplanes ever built. The first one flew in 1935. More than 10,000 were built, and a number of these are still in regular use.

The DC-3 is considered one of the most reliable airplanes ever built. This one disappeared, and no one knows what happened to it.

In 1963, a cargo ship called the *Marine Sulphur Queen* left Texas. The vessel was bound for Baltimore, Maryland. It never arrived. Searchers found a few small pieces of wreckage from the ship near Florida, but there

Seaman Earnest Randolph Crammer was one of more than 300 U.S. Navy personnel who vanished along with the *Cyclops*. Not everyone is convinced that the Bermuda Triangle caused the ship to disappear. One theory for its loss is that the cargo shifted suddenly during a severe storm, causing the ship to capsize. Another is that she was sunk by a German submarine. World War I was still raging at that time. It's not surprising that no distress call was received from the ship. At that time, shipboard emergency communications were still in their infancy.

were no other traces. Thirteen years later, another cargo ship, the *Sylvia L. Ossa,* vanished near Bermuda. Both vessels were nearly 600 feet long.

Not all stories end tragically. Pilot Bruce Gernon often flew between the Bahama (bah-HAH-mah) Islands and Florida. The Bahamas lie between Puerto Rico and Miami. Gernon's trip normally took 75 minutes. On December 4, 1970, Gernon took off from the Bahamas. Soon he encountered a cigar-shaped cloud. He climbed to get around it, but the cloud kept growing. It surrounded his airplane. There was a tunnel in the middle, and Gernon flew through it. He found himself moving very fast. His compass spun wildly. When he emerged, he was near his destination. The trip took only 47 minutes. He had also used much less fuel than usual.

Rogue waves are much larger than normal and appear without warning. The highest recorded rogue wave was an estimated 112 feet—taller than a ten-story building.

CHAPTER
FOUR

Some Explanations

People who have written about the Bermuda Triangle offer many reasons for the mysterious disappearances. Some reasons seem more likely than others.

Natural causes are one group of explanations. They include high winds, sudden storms, and strong currents. Rogue waves are huge waves up to 100 feet high that seem to come out of nowhere. They can capsize even big ships in a matter of moments.

Human error is another possible reason. Even experienced pilots can make mistakes. People's senses don't always give correct information, especially at night. A pilot may think he is flying level when he is actually diving. He may fly straight into the ocean.

19

Another theory involves **methane** gas. When dead sea animals and plants **decompose**, they create methane. Sometimes huge bubbles of methane gas are released. They float to the surface and pop, creating holes in the surface of the water. If a ship passes when a bubble pops, the ship falls into the hole. Water instantly covers the ship and sinks it.

Meanwhile, the gas continues to rise, forming a cloud. Methane burns easily. If an

Methane gas forms in the ocean where dead plants and animals break down. Some scientists believe that a great deal of methane lies under the sea. It could become a major source of fuel and energy.

airplane flies through the cloud, it could **ignite** the gas and explode. The airplane would either burn in the air or crash.

Some explanations are more far-fetched. For example, some writers believe that the famous "lost city" of Atlantis may be to blame. They say Atlantis was a large island that lay off the coast of Florida. Somehow it sank. They

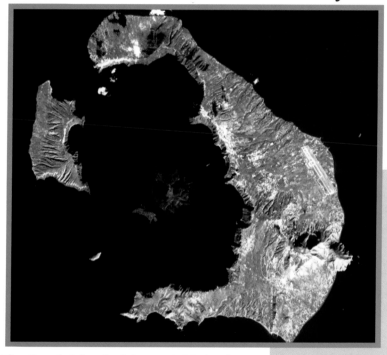

The Greek island of Santorini is in the Mediterranean Sea. Some people believe that the lost island of Atlantis was part of Santorini. Atlantis was "lost" when a volcanic eruption destroyed the center of the island. Others believe Atlantis was in the Atlantic Ocean, close to Florida.

21

believe its energy came from **crystals**, and the crystals are still at the bottom of the sea. If they are, these crystals could interfere with equipment on ships and airplanes.

Wormholes are another explanation. A wormhole is like a gateway that connects distant points in time or space. A plane or ship traveling through one of these tunnels can

A wormhole may bend space and time to increase the speed of travel between two points. No one has ever seen a wormhole. This is one artist's idea of what one might look like.

supposedly reach another time or another universe.

Some people believe in unidentified flying objects (UFOs). UFOs, or "flying saucers," are said to carry beings from outer space. These beings might be taking ships and airplanes from the Earth—at the Bermuda Triangle.

The explanations go on and on. Some ships may have disappeared after a **mutiny**. Ships lost during wartime may have been sunk by submarines. Pirates may have captured others. A few people even blame sea monsters.

In the end, though, none of the explanations answer all the questions. The mystery remains a mystery.

The headquarters of Lloyd's of London, one of the world's most famous insurance companies. It specializes in insuring large ships. Its origins go back to the late 1600s in a London coffeehouse owned by Edward Lloyd. Lloyd's does not see the Bermuda Triangle as especially dangerous.

Is the Bermuda Triangle Real?

Although many people believe there are **supernatural** forces at work in the Bermuda Triangle, others say there is nothing special about the area. The U.S. government, Coast Guard, and Navy treat the Bermuda Triangle as they would any other place on earth. The triangle is not identified on official U.S. maps of the area.

Insurance companies also do not seem to think the Bermuda Triangle is a risky area for travel. These companies figure out what to charge customers by the amount of risk involved. For example, a man who is 70 is more likely to die soon than a man who is 20.

It is a greater risk to insure the older man. His insurance rates are much higher.

Lloyd's of London is a famous company that insures ships. Lloyd's has studied stories about the Bermuda Triangle. The company doesn't raise its rates for ships that pass through the area. It says the triangle is no more risky than any other part of the world's oceans.

Doubters say the disappearance of Flight 19 isn't such a mystery. They say that the planes simply got lost, then ran out of fuel. They add that the search plane didn't just vanish. Someone on a ship saw an explosion at the exact spot where the search plane would have been.

There are other reasons for doubt. Some incidents that believers claim happened inside the triangle happened outside it. Other incidents happened during severe storms. Yet believers claim the incidents happened in good weather.

Still, a lot of people believe there are many more unexplained disappearances inside the Bermuda Triangle than anywhere else in the

world. They say boats and airplanes still vanish there every year. Although the U.S. Coast Guard says the area is "imaginery," natural causes can't explain all of these disappearances.

Believers also say some people, like Bruce Gernon, have had firsthand experience with mysterious forces inside the triangle. Most of these witnesses, however, don't want to talk about their experiences. They are afraid other people will laugh at them.

Science is always uncovering new things about the world and how it works. Perhaps someday we will know for sure about the Bermuda Triangle. Until then, people will continue to wonder about it.

CHRONOLOGY

1492 Christopher Columbus reports a fireball in the sky and strange compass movements as he nears land in the New World.

1609 English sailing ship *Sea Venture* is wrecked in a storm off Bermuda.

1814 U.S. Navy ship USS *Wasp* disappears.

1843 U.S. Navy ship USS *Grampus* and crew of 48 disappear.

1855 British passenger ship *City of Glasgow* disappears, carrying 400 passengers and crew of more than 80.

1872 Sailing ship *Mary Celeste* is found drifting with no sign of the ten people who had been aboard.

1880 British naval training ship HMS *Atalanta* disappears with more than 300 people aboard.

1909 Joshua Slocum, the first man to sail around the world by himself, and his boat *Spray* disappear.

1918 USS *Cyclops* vanishes with more than 300 men.

1941 USS *Proteus* and USS *Nereus*, sister ships to USS *Cyclops*, disappear.

1945 Five planes on training mission Flight 19 disappear.

1948 *Star Tiger* and Miami-bound DC-3 both disappear.

1949 *Star Ariel* disappears.

1950 E.V.W. Jones writes about mysterious disappearances.

1952 Writer George X. Sand maps out the mysterious triangle.

1963 Cargo ship *Marine Sulphur Queen* disappears with crew of 39.

1964 Writer Vincent Gaddis is first to use name "Bermuda Triangle."

1974 Charles Berlitz's *The Bermuda Triangle* becomes a best-selling book.

1975 Lawrence Kusche's *The Bermuda Triangle Mystery—Solved* seeks to prove that the mysterious disappearances all have natural causes.

1976 Ore carrier *Sylvia Ossa* and crew of 37 disappear.

1978 Douglas DC-3 N407D disappears on its way to Cuba.

1990s Several large jetliners make emergency landings due to unexpected turbulence.

2004 Gian J. Quasar writes *Into the Bermuda Triangle,* which updates evidence for the Bermuda Triangle.

FIND OUT MORE

Books

Donkin, Andrew. *DK Readers: Bermuda Triangle.* New York: DK Children, 2000.

Innes, Brian. *Unsolved Mysteries: The Bermuda Triangle.* Austin, Texas: Raintree Steck-Vaughn, 1999.

Oxlade, Chris. *The Mystery of the Bermuda Triangle.* Chicago: Heinemann Library, 2000.

Rosenberg, Aaron. *Unsolved Mysteries: The Bermuda Triangle.* New York: The Rosen Publishing Group, 2002.

Works Consulted

Berlitz, Charles. *The Bermuda Triangle.* New York: Doubleday, 1974.

Kusche, Lawrence David. *The Bermuda Triangle Mystery— Solved.* New York: HarperCollins, 1975.

Quasar, Gian. *Into the Bermuda Triangle.* New York: International Marine/Ragged Mountain Press, 2004.

U.S. Coast Guard and U.S. Navy. "Bermuda Triangle Fact Sheet." http://www.history.navy.mil/faqs/faq8-1.htm

On the Internet

Scary Places Part 4: The Bermuda Triangle
http://www.kidzworld.com/site/p1136.htm

The Haunted Doghouse
http://www.haunteddoghouse.com/The_Bermuda_Tr.html

The Unnatural Museum. "The Un-Mystery of the Bermuda Triangle."
http://www.unmuseum.org/triangle.htm

Why Is the Bermuda Triangle Considered Mysterious?
http://www.4to40.com/earth/geography/
index.asp?article=earth_geography_bermudatriangle

GLOSSARY

crystals (KRIH-stuls)—clear, six-sided pieces of quartz (KWORTS) that can interfere with electrical fields.

decompose (dee-kum-POHZ)—rot, break down.

doubters (DOW-turs)—people who don't believe that something is true.

ignite (ig-NYT)—light on fire.

legend (LEH-jend)—a well-known extraordinary story whose truth cannot be proved.

methane (MEH-thayn)—a colorless, odorless, and flammable gas formed when certain substances decompose.

mutiny (MYOOT-nee)—to rebel against an established authority, such as the captain of a ship.

supernatural (SOO-per-NAA-chuh-rul)—something beyond ordinary experience or observation.

triangular (try-ANG-yoo-lur)—in the shape of a triangle.

INDEX

Atlantis 21

Bahama Islands 17

Baltimore, Maryland
  15

Barbados 13

Berlitz, Charles 11, 13

Bermuda 9, 10, 12,
  13

Bermuda Triangle,
  map of 12
  naming of 9–10

Caribbean Sea 13

Columbus, Christopher
  11, 12

Crammer, Earnest
  Randolph 16

crystals 22

Cyclops, USS 13, 14,
  16

DC-3 14, 15

Flight 19 4, 5–7, 8, 26

Florida 9, 15, 17, 21

Florida Keys 6

Fort Lauderdale, Florida
  4, 5

Gaddis, Vincent 10

Gernon, Bruce 17, 27

Gulf of Mexico 6

Jones, E.V.W. 9

Lloyd's of London 24,
  26

Marine Sulphur Queen
  15

methane gas 20

Miami, Florida 6, 8,
  12, 14

Puerto Rico 9, 11, 12,
  14

rogue waves 18, 19

Sand, George X. 9

Santorini Island 21

Star Ariel 14

Star Tiger 13

Sylvia L. Ossa 17

Taylor, Charles 5, 6, 7

Titler, Dale Milton 10

torpedo bombers 4,
  5, 8

UFOs 23

wormholes 22–23